EXPLORER BOOKS

FIRE

by Jean Waricha

Published by The Trumpet Club
1540 Broadway, New York, New York 10036

Copyright © 1992 Parachute Press, Inc.

ISBN 0-440-84866-0

Printed in the United States of America

November 1992

3   5   7   9   10   8   6   4   2

CWO

PHOTOGRAPH CREDITS

p. 21: top, AP/Wide World Photos; *bottom,* AP/Wide World Photos; *p. 22: top,*
AP/Wide World Photos; *bottom,* AP/Wide World Photos; *p. 23: top,* Ray
Hellriegel/Globe Photos; *bottom,* The Bettmann Archive; *p. 24: top,* Culver
Pictures; *bottom,* Culver Pictures; *p. 25: top,* UPI/Bettmann Newsphotos;
bottom, UPI/Bettmann Newsphotos; *p. 26: top,* AP/Wide World Photos;
bottom, UPI/Bettmann Newsphotos; *p. 27: top,* AP/Wide World Photos;
bottom, AP/Wide World Photos; *p. 28: AP / Wide World Photos.*

Cover: © 1989 Comstock, Inc./Jim Pickerell

To the Monroe School librarians
for all their help

Contents

1

Where Does Fire Come From?

No one knows for sure how fire was first discovered. We do know, however, that fire has been in existence since the world began. From ancient to modern times, people have been fascinated by its mystery.

Fire must have seemed like magic to the earliest humans. Cave men and women probably saw fire caused by lightning strikes and volcanic eruptions. It probably frightened them. To help them understand where fire came from, people created legends to explain it.

According to a story told by the Creek Indians, who lived in the southeastern United States about 500 years ago, the first people on Earth did not know how to make fire. In the winter it would get so cold that the people would freeze into human ice cubes.

One day lightning struck a tree on a nearby island. People could see the fire burning, but they couldn't get to it. At night they watched the animals dance around the fire to keep warm. The people envied the animals. They wanted this fire.

1

The rabbit felt sorry for the freezing people and decided to help them. So one night he dipped his tail in tar and swam to the island. The rabbit waited until the other animals began to dance. Then he joined them. Suddenly he bent backward over the fire and a flame caught onto his fur. Carrying the fire on his tail, he swam back across the water, bringing fire to the people.

Flint Stones

Cave men and women probably discovered how to make fire by accident. It is believed that lightning caused the first fires. Early man may have overcome his fear and picked up a burning stick. Or he may have figured out how to keep a red-hot coal burning. In a cave in southern France, scientists found a fireplace with ashes packed 22 feet deep. The cave dwellers, who lived there 400,000 years ago, must have kept this fire alive for several generations to build such a thick ash deposit.

Soon man began to think about ways of making fire whenever he needed it. One of the earliest methods probably involved rubbing two pieces of wood together. As the wood became warmer from the rubbing, it would start to glow, and a person could blow on it to create a flame. Or people may have banged two pieces of pyrite (commonly called *flint stones*) together to make sparks.

We do know that early man made his tools from

stone by chipping or striking them together. If two flint stones are struck together, tiny sparks of glowing stone are produced. These sparks disappear quickly when they cool. However, if a spark falls onto some tinder—dry grass or wood shavings—a fire can start. At first these fires may have begun by accident, but perhaps after seeing fires start so often, prehistoric people learned how to make them whenever they needed to. But first they had to find and save flint stones, for only these stones produce sparks that cause fire.

By the time people learned to make fire, it was already an important part of everyday life. Stone Age hunters who lived nearly 700,000 years ago sat around fireplaces.

Early fireplaces were nothing more than a simple pile of sticks lying on the ground. Later, people dug a shallow pit and surrounded it with stones to contain the flames. Most fires burned wood or animal bones, but scientists have found evidence in one Stone Age fireplace of coal being used for fuel.

Fire warmed men's and women's overnight camps and winter cave dwellings. Until cave people learned to control fire, they could only live in warm climates. Fire made it possible for them to live in northern climates during the winter.

Fire also gave people light. For cave people, the knowledge of fire made their days longer. They had more time to make tools, plan hunts, and sit around a fire telling stories. It also made their lives safer.

Scientists believe that firelight inside the caves may have helped scare off animals that hunt at night.

No one knows how people got the idea of cooking meat in the fire. Scientists have found evidence of large mammal bones in the fireplaces of Stone Age hunters in Yugoslavia. This could mean that cave men and women invented barbecued meat nearly 400,000 years ago!

Roast meat was an important early discovery. Cooked meat not only tastes better than raw meat, it is easier to eat—less effort is required to chew it. A result of eating cooked meat was a change in man's appearance. Early man had wide jaws and large teeth. Since cave men and women no longer had to chew their meat so hard once they started cooking it, eventually their teeth became smaller and their jaws became shorter.

Once man had become a master at making fire, he began to wonder what exactly was fire? What caused it? Why did it give off heat and light?

What Is Fire?

Fire is a chemical process in which fuel and oxygen from the air are combined by heat. Heat, a form of energy, is what causes the chemical reaction that starts a fire. To make the chemical reaction occur, flammable material must be heated until it reaches its ignition temperature, or *kindling point* (as when two sticks are rubbed together). This is the temperature at which it will start to burn in the air.

A fire takes in oxygen and gives out carbon dioxide, just as we do. When the fire takes in oxygen rapidly, a flame is the result. The smoke created by the chemical reaction of fire is made of water and *carbon dioxide.*

Sometimes there can be a fire even without a flame. If fuel combines with oxygen *very* slowly, the heat is carried away by the air and no light is given out. An example of a fire without a flame is rust.

Fires can sometimes light themselves. If oily rags are piled together, for instance, heat can build up in the rags. What happens is that air cannot circulate to carry away the heat. The heat and the oil (the fuel) combine in a chemical reaction that causes the rags to ignite. Then the rags burst into flames. This is called *spontaneous combustion,* and it happens when more heat is being produced than can escape into the atmosphere.

Some things just won't burn. Water and sand can't ignite because they are already burned. Water is the result of a chemical reaction between hydrogen and oxygen. When these two elements are heated, they burn together to make water. Sand can't burn either—it is burned silicon.

When fire is under control, it is an important part of our lives. We use its heat to cook food, warm our homes, move our cars—and to make plastic, paper, and other important materials. We burn trash and other waste materials. Fire can also destroy harmful germs. Holding a needle in a flame is one way to sterilize it before removing a splinter from your finger.

However, when fire is uncontrolled, it is one of the most destructive forces on Earth.

2

Two Famous Fires

The Great Chicago Fire

On the night of October 8, 1871, the flames from one lamp on the west side of Chicago set off a fire that nearly destroyed the city. In the 1870's Chicago was a city of wood—most of its buildings and even the sidewalks were wooden. Although it was a city of 300,000 people, it had fewer than 200 firefighters. Insurance companies often refused to insure the buildings—they said the city was one big pile of kindling wood. The T-shaped Chicago River divided the city into three sections. In the north were residential houses and heavy industry along the waterfront; the commercial center was in the south; and in the west were small one- and two-story houses.

The O'Leary family lived in the western section. Patrick O'Leary and his wife, Catherine, were about 35 years old, and had five children. They owned two small wooden cottages; they rented out the front one and lived in the back one. Near their cottage was a barn from which they ran a milk route.

According to Mrs. O'Leary, she went to her barn around 8:30 that evening to get milk for a neighbor's party. Setting her lamp on the floor, she tried to milk the cow, but the cow kicked over the lamp, and the burning kerosene set fire to the straw. Though her screams brought neighbors who tried to put out the fire, the entire barn was soon burning.

Ten minutes later, unable to stop the blaze, a neighbor ran to an alarm box—but it had been locked to prevent false alarms. The owner of a nearby store, who had a key, ran home to get it. When the alarm was finally pulled, for some reason it didn't ring at the station house. When a fire watcher finally noticed the fire, he estimated it was three blocks away from the O'Learys—so he sent the firefighters to the wrong place. By this time the fire had already been burning out of control for 45 minutes. When a second alarm was sounded, the alarm system still did not work.

Two engine companies finally arrived at the scene of the fire, but they faced many problems. Their fire hoses caught fire, the water pumps broke, and the water pressure went flat. A forceful wind from the southwest blew burning bits of wood blocks ahead of the fire. The heat was so intense that in order to get near the fire the firefighters had to cool the ground in front of them with water.

However, the firemen thought some progress was being made—until they heard that Saint Paul's Roman Catholic Church, several blocks away, had caught fire. Over 30 houses were now burning between the O'Learys and the church. Equipment had to be sent from the main fire to the one at the church. At this point no one believed that either fire could be contained.

Two four-story wooden factories next to the church were soon in flames. Thousands of Chicagoans ran to the area to see the fire. Mobs broke into taverns to steal kegs of beer, which they rolled into the street.

Half an hour later, the fire jumped the Chicago River to the southern part of the city, where the gas company was: the wind had carried pieces of burning wood across the river. The lights in the city went out as workers quickly shut off the gas, letting it drain into the sewers to prevent a huge explosion. But the plan backfired—the gas ignited from the sewers.

It has been estimated that the heat of the fire rose as high as 3,000 degrees Fahrenheit. At this heat the metal of the trolley tracks started to melt and curl.

Mayor Roswell B. Mason ordered the firefighters to try stopping the fire by blowing up buildings. He thought that this would deprive the fire of fuel. Three blocks of buildings were blown up, but it didn't help.

Panicking, the mayor sent telegraph messages to nearby cities: "Send help! Chicago in flames!" Within hours more than twenty-five engines from eight states were speeding to Chicago on railroad flatcars.

It seemed as if nothing could stop the fire. It devoured the Tremont House, where Abraham Lincoln and Stephen A. Douglas had had their famous debates, and it destroyed the Chicago *Times* Building, where workers were preparing a story about the fire. In one Chicago bank it turned 2 million dollars in cash into ashes.

The city was in a panic as thousands fled over burning bridges. Looters stole fire horses, forcing firemen to pull their own wagons. By 3:20 a.m. the city's 38-million-gallon waterworks, the first built in the United States, was burning in the north division. Everyone hoped it could still pump water to the fires, but when a section of the roof collapsed on the machinery, it stopped working.

By dawn, thousands of people were running to the shores of Lake Michigan. To escape the heat and smoke, they buried their cows and children in the sand up to their necks and ran to the lake for cooling water.

At noon, the fire swept into Lincoln Park and destroyed the Chicago bank building, and along with it Lincoln's walking stick and the original Emancipation Proclamation.

The fire continued to burn—it seemed as if the devastation would never end. Then at 11:00 p.m. on October 10, more than two days after the fire started, it began to rain. At 3:00 a.m. the next day, a hard rain drenched the ruins. The Great Chicago Fire was over. The rain had put out the blaze.

Between 150 and 300 people died—the exact

number isn't known. Over 100,000 of the city's 200,000 citizens were left homeless. The entire center of the city was destroyed: 17,450 buildings— including thousands of homes and hundreds of factories and stores—had simply burned down. Property loss was estimated at about $200 million, only $88 million of which was insured. Strangely, one of the houses that did survive was one of the O'Leary's cottages.

When news of the fire reached the rest of the world, money, food, and clothing poured into Chicago. Immediately the people began to rebuild, and the newspapers proclaimed, "Chicago will rise again!" A new and beautiful city rose from the ruins of the old.

A tragic lesson had been learned from the Great Chicago Fire. New buildings were made fireproof— constructed from materials other than wood that wouldn't catch fire. Sprinkler systems were installed, and firefighting methods were improved, as was the city's system for transporting water to fires.

The Peshtigo Fire

In 1871 Peshtigo was a thriving lumber town of 2,000 people, located in the middle of a forest in northwestern Wisconsin. Wood products produced in Peshtigo were sent by railroad to Chicago, and then sold throughout the world.

The summer of 1871 had been an unusually hot one. In September only a light drizzle had fallen in and around the city. By October the pine trees were starting to lose their needles and turn brown.

Small fires broke out in the peat bogs around Peshtigo, and dark smoke began to fill the air. The fires caused the air to get unusually hot—the people called it "oven" hot. At night an orange glow could be seen rising from the swamplands. The citizens of Peshtigo began to worry and feel uneasy.

On October 8 a small fire started in the forest area west of the town. As the day went on, smoke filled the air and blotted out the sun. Telegraph lines outside Peshtigo caught fire and burned, leaving the people without a link to the outside world. Major roads leading out of the town, which were made of wooden logs, also caught fire.

By early evening the loud and continuous roar of the blaze could be heard from the woods. By 9:30 that night fire had swallowed the town. First, the tops of the trees on the outskirts caught fire. Then the town was showered by sparks that started more fires.

Within minutes the blaze became a truly monstrous fire that had the town surrounded. A blast of super-hot air shook every building. Houses, barns, stores, trees, and grass burst into flames. But it wasn't just the flames that were deadly. Gases sucked out of the swamps now exploded in the air. The force of the wind tore weaker houses apart. The people were trapped, not really knowing what to do. The town was isolated.

The smartest ran for the Peshtigo River. They

stood neck deep in the river, dunking their heads in the water to escape from falling embers or sparks. They would stay under as long as possible to escape the heat, the smoke, the flames—then they would raise their heads for air.

Those who were not so lucky died from *asphyxiation*—they lacked enough oxygen to breathe. The fire used up so much oxygen that there wasn't enough left for the people.

By dawn the next day, the town no longer existed. Thirteen hundred people died. Of the town's 400 buildings, only a single wall of *one* house remained, and 400 farms were destroyed. The fire kept going and wiped out over a million acres of timberland. The next day, cooling rains fell on Peshtigo. But the rain was too late to save lives—it cooled only the ashes.

The Peshtigo fire was surely one of the deadliest fires ever to strike the United States. Yet it received little newspaper coverage. Why? Because it occurred on October 8, 1871—the very same day as the Great Chicago Fire. People were much more interested in the destruction of a well-known city than that of a small town.

3

Disasters That Brought Change

It was payday on Saturday, March 25, 1911, for the young men and women who worked at the Triangle Shirtwaist Factory. After working over thirteen hours a day, six days a week, they were looking forward to Sunday—their one day off. But by closing time, 145 of them were dead.

"Don't Jump!"

The Triangle Shirtwaist Factory Fire of 1911 didn't have to happen. The factory, located on the eighth, ninth, and tenth floors of the Asch building on the corner of Washington Place and Greene Street in New York City, was a known firetrap. Fire experts had given repeated warnings to Joseph J. Asch, one of the building's owners, that the fire escape didn't reach all the way to the ground. There was no sprinkler system and no fire drill education. Despite frequent strikes by workers to make changes, the owners refused to listen. The men and women who worked at the factory were afraid they would lose their jobs, so they gave up the fight for safer working conditions.

The blouse factory had wooden windows and floors. There were only two staircases, instead of the regulation three, because the architect argued that the single fire escape counted as the third staircase.

One stairway was located on Greene Street, the other on Washington Place. The fire escape was also on Greene Street. The Greene Street stairway was the only one with an exit to the roof—the Washington Place stairway went up only to the tenth floor. The fire escape was located at the rear of the building and reached down only to the second floor above an enclosed courtyard.

A total of 500 people, mostly women, worked on the eighth and ninth floors. The women worked on sewing machines in tightly packed rows. A small number of men oiled the machines and replaced broken parts. On March 25, near closing time, the tables were covered with tissue-paper patterns, and finished blouses hung from the ceiling. A small fire started in a wastepaper basket on the eighth floor, perhaps from a cigarette. The fire ignited the overhead blouses.

Terrified men and women rushed to the elevators and pushed against the doors. But the elevators could only accommodate about twelve people at a time. Some jumped into the elevator shaft, trying to land on top of the car as it made its way down. A few of those people somehow survived. Others found the fire escape, which was dangerously close to the flames. While many of them suffered burns, most of the people on the eighth floor were able to escape.

Someone on the eighth floor found a fire hose and tried to put out the flames. However, the hoses had been allowed to rot and the water valves were rusted, so they couldn't be used. Someone else tried to warn the women on the ninth and tenth floors, but the telephone on the ninth floor didn't work. The call went through only to the tenth floor, where the business and shipping offices were located. The women on the ninth floor continued to work, unaware of the chaos below them.

There were seventy people on the tenth floor. They decided that the quickest way out was to use the Greene Street stairs to the roof. Only one of them died.

When the people on the ninth floor finally realized what was happening, they rushed to the door of the Washington Place stairs. It was locked! The door was kept locked because the owners thought the women might be stealing materials. In fact, someone was supposed to check their purses before they left each night. Next many of them tried to use the Greene Street fire escape but by then it was clogged with people. The fire had become so intense that the flames shooting out of the building made the metal fire escape bend out of shape. With so much weight on it, the fire escape buckled and the people on it fell to the ground. The remaining people were trapped. Spectators on the street yelled, "Don't jump! Don't jump!" But many became frightened and jumped out the ninth-floor windows to their death. Other people jumped into fire nets, but the force of so many bodies landing at once tore the nets from the firefighters' hands.

The Hook and Ladder Company, which had the longest ladder in the New York City Fire Department, rushed to the scene of the fire. But their ladder reached only as high as the sixth floor. The fire chief ordered the men to aim high-pressure hoses at women near the windows to cool them down from the intense heat.

Finally, the firefighters raced up the ten flights of stairs to fight the fire with hand extinguishers and axes. Within 20 minutes, they had put the fire out. But 145 men and women out of 570 had already been killed.

A crowd of more than 10,000 watched the tragedy in horror. The public was outraged and demanded changes. On Wednesday, April 5, a massive public funeral was held. Despite a heavy rain, more than 100,000 people marched.

The owners of the factory were charged with first- and second-degree manslaughter and brought to trial. The jury found them *not* guilty. Many of the jurors had no doubt that the door leading to the Washington Place stairs had been locked. But they felt that it couldn't be murder if employees had agreed to work behind a locked door. And no one could prove that the men and women *didn't* know the doors were locked. Then relatives of the victims sued the owners and won—but the average settlement was only $75.

The tragedy of the Triangle Shirtwaist Factory Fire helped to bring about new fire laws. Buildings now had to have sprinkler systems, and fire marshals inspected all factories. *Sweatshops* (a slang term for factories where workers are employed for long hours and low wages under unhealthy conditions) were reformed. After the Triangle fire, the International Ladies' Garment Workers' Union became much more powerful. One of its main purposes was to make sure such a tragedy as the Triangle fire never happened again.

The Cocoanut Grove Fire

Though it was made of brick and believed to be fireproof, the Cocoanut Grove Nightclub in Boston burned to the ground on November 28, 1942. On that night there was a big party planned for the Boston College football team. When the team lost to Holy Cross, many of the spectators decided to go ahead and celebrate at the nightclub anyway. The players had planned to be at the party, but after their loss they decided to go home—a decision that probably saved their lives.

About 1,000 people crowded into the club, which had a maximum capacity of 600. There were two floors—the street level and the basement level. The club was decorated with paper palm trees and bamboo groves to make it look like a South Sea island.

Blue satin cloth was spread across the ceiling to resemble the sky. In Melody Lounge, a part of the club downstairs, a light bulb burned out. At about 10:00 p.m., a worker tried to replace it. He couldn't find the light socket, so he lit a match. The match flared up and accidentally ignited one of the paper palm trees. The fire quickly jumped to the cloth-covered ceiling and spread rapidly.

Someone shouted "Fire!" Panicking, people in the basement ran for the stairs to the street-level exit. In the midst of the pushing and shoving, the lights went out. Some people managed to run out through the basement kitchen, while others hid inside a giant walk-in refrigerator. A few climbed through the kitchen windows to a courtyard outside. Those who made it to the door of the upstairs lounge found themselves trapped—the exit door was locked to make sure no one entered the club without paying the entry fee, or left without paying the bar bill. Over 200 people were later found dead by this door.

The fire quickly spread throughout the club. Frantic people ran to the revolving door at the street-level entrance, which was soon jammed. When firefighters arrived, the pile of people at this exit prevented them from getting inside. Other people discovered a second street-level door, while some escaped through a courtyard entrance.

The firemen found other exits that people in the club hadn't—one was hidden by heavy decorative drapes. Drapes also covered many street-level windows, and so people didn't even know they were there—if they had, they could have broken them to get out.

The firefighters soon had the fire under control. It lasted only 12 minutes, but it killed 491 people and injured 166. The angry public demanded to know why it had happened. Investigation revealed that the club's wiring had been done by an unlicensed electrician, and that building codes had been violated. It was decided that the owner, Barnett Welansky, knew about these problems. He was sentenced to 12 to 15 years in jail for manslaughter. The contractor who built one of the lounges was also sentenced to 2 years on a charge of conspiracy to violate building codes.

As a result of the Cocoanut Grove Fire, the building codes were updated, and insurance companies increased their research on fireproof materials. But the improvements were too late for the many victims of the tragedy at Cocoanut Grove.

This drawing from over 100 years ago shows thousands of people fleeing the downtown area of the city during the Great Chicago Fire of October 8, 1871.

After the fire, downtown Chicago lay in ruins. The charred skeleton of the Chicago Courthouse remained standing (center of photograph).

This painting, which hangs on the wall of the Peshtigo Fire Museum, shows residents fleeing from the fire to the Peshtigo River.

Spectators run as the Hindenburg bursts into flames while trying to land on May 6, 1937, in Lakehurst, New Jersey.

During the 1860's, horse-drawn steam engines were used to fight fires in large American cities.

Motorized fire engines took the place of horse-drawn engines in the early 1900's. Here a fire truck with a gas motor engine pulls a pump and hose truck.

Women trapped by the Triangle Shirtwaist Factory Fire of 1911 struggled to reach the roof of the building by way of the fire escape.

The Triangle Shirtwaist Factory fire escape buckled from the intense heat, and many people fell to their deaths.

The remains of Boston's Cocoanut Grove Nightclub after the 1942 fire that killed 491 of the estimated 1,000 people who were there that night.

A view of the fire damage inside Cocoanut Grove Nightclub after the bodies of the victims were removed.

Smoke jumpers parachute from a DC-3 during a forest fire-fighter training session in Idaho.

An army helicopter pre-pares to drop water on Yellowstone National Park on August 31, 1988. The smoke is so thick it almost blocks out the sun.

Christa McAuliffe, the first civilian chosen to travel in space, is honored by a parade in her hometown of Concord, New Hampshire, in 1985, the day after she was picked for the space mission.

The Challenger space shuttle explodes on January 28, 1986, shortly after lift-off from the Kennedy Space Center in Florida. Seven crew members, including Christa McAuliffe, were aboard.

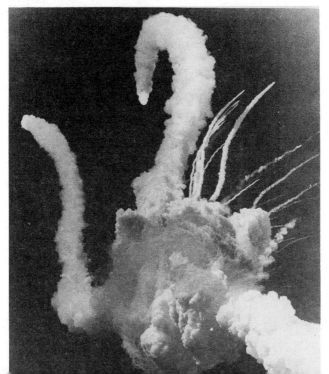

Oil-field workers in Kuwait struggle to save a burning oil well by installing a pipe that will transport the oil after the fire is extinguished.

4

Fighting Fires

Ever since people began living in cities, fire has been an enemy to be dealt with. Early cities consisted of wooden buildings built close together on narrow streets. The ancient city of Knossos, capital of Crete, burned to the ground 3,000 years ago. Carthage, a city of over a million people in North Africa, was reduced to ashes in 800 B.C. In both of these fires, people were helpless because they had no idea how to fight a fire. It wasn't until Roman times that people began to think of organized solutions.

Ctesibius of Alexandria, who lived in the Roman Empire around 200 B.C., realized that the best way to put out a fire was to use air to propel water onto the flames. He constructed a hose made from the intestines of an ox and connected it to the first water pump in history. Ctesibius's water pump was shaped like an upside-down U. Two pistons, attached at the top by a crossbar, fit snugly into a brass cylinder-shaped casing, and stood in a tub of water. When the pistons were pulled up and down, water rose in one cylinder and air rose in the other.

As long as the tub was kept full of water, the air forced the water out in spurts.

The Romans organized the very first fire department. These firefighters called themselves the "Corps of Vigils." The corps was set up like a small military group. They were equipped with ladders, ropes, brooms, nets, axes, and of course, the Ctesibius pump. During the Golden Age of Rome, around A.D. 100, there were over 10,000 men in the Roman fire department!

When the Roman Empire fell in about A.D. 500, the Ctesibius pump was lost. However, Ctesibius's pump was the basic principle behind every fire engine for more than 2,000 years—until the 1920's. That's when the first gas-powered fire engines were put into use.

Instead of developing firefighting methods, people of the Middle Ages in Europe were more concerned with fire prevention. Every home had to have a barrel of water outside the door, and homes were required to douse their hearths with water at night. In the 1500's, wooden chimneys were outlawed in Europe, and hearths had to be made of iron or some other fireproof material.

"Throw Out Your Buckets!"

In colonial America, chimneys were the chief cause of fire. At that time chimneys were made of wood, with layers of mud inside to protect it from catching fire. Too often the mud would dry out or chip off, and the fireplace would catch fire. Sparks from the fire frequently landed on the thatched roofs of nearby houses. America's first fire regulations were the result of such disasters.

The earliest building construction regulations were set by Peter Stuyvesant in New Amsterdam (later New York City) in 1648. He outlawed wooden chimneys and appointed four fire wardens to inspect all chimneys. Owners were fined if a fire occurred in their home. The fines were used to buy ladders, hooks, and water buckets.

Colonial towns also set up a night watch consisting of eight men. These men, known as *prowlers,* patrolled the streets from nine in the evening until dawn. When a prowler spotted a fire he would shake a heavy wooden rattle over his head and shout "Fire! Throw out your buckets!" When the other prowlers heard the rattle they would take up the cry and shake their rattles. Since few people could sleep with this racket going on, everyone would get up, throw their empty fire buckets out the window, get dressed, and run to help put out the fire.

The prowlers would head for the town pump and start to fill the buckets to form a *bucket brigade*. A bucket brigade is made up of two lines of people stretched out from the pump to the fire. Men passed the water-filled buckets out, and women and children passed empty buckets back again. Buckets were transferred back and forth until the fire was put out—or more often until the house burned down.

This community firefighting effort continued until the 1700's, when Benjamin Franklin popularized the idea of the organized volunteer fire department. In 1736 his Union Fire Company of Philadelphia began fighting fires. Soon all major American cities were organizing volunteer fire departments.

The First Fire Engines

In colonial days hand pumps were used that had to be pulled or carried to a fire. Fire engines are believed to have been invented in Germany, but the Richard Newsham pumper, which was invented in England in 1725, was the first engine exported to America. This was the first pumper to shoot a continuous stream of water on a fire. It had a design similar to the Ctesibius pump, though it had a gooseneck nozzle that attached to the water opening, and the water was pumped by manually operated handles. There was one little problem with these engines, though—their wheels did not pivot, so to turn the engine around a corner, firefighters actually had to pick it up and swing it around!

Hoses

The Newsham pumper could carry up to 200 feet of leather hose. Until 1807 these hoses were made of leather stitched together the way shoemakers made boots. But stitched hoses leaked badly and burst open from high water pressure. James Sellers and

Abraham L. Pennock of Philadelphia came up with a solution: They used metal rivets instead of stitches to hold the seams together.

The hoses were between 40 and 50 feet long and weighed more than 84 pounds. The riveted hose was immediately popular—but not perfect. It wasn't flexible and needed special care so it wouldn't rot or crack. In 1839 Charles Goodyear discovered a process called *vulcanization,* a way to treat crude rubber with chemicals and heat it until it became stronger and more elastic. This led to the growth of the rubber industry, and later that same year people started using rubber to make hoses, as they still do today.

Fire Hydrants and Alarms

As American cities grew in the 1800's, firefighters had two major problems: There was still no reliable fire alarm system, and getting water to a fire site was not always easy. The critical moments occur during the first few minutes after a fire starts. If the firefighters don't get to a fire fast, it is much harder to stop and can burn out of control.

Samuel B. Morse's invention of the telegraph in 1844 helped to give firemen a much faster and more accurate alarm system. In 1852 Dr. William F. Channing of Boston designed a system of metal boxes that used telegraph signals. When someone pulled a handle on the box, the location of the box would be transmitted to a central office. The central office would then tap out the location of the fire and the nearest firehouse. Firefighters could reach the fire in a matter of minutes.

The next problem to be solved was how to get large quantities of water to the fire—enough to put it out before it got out of control.

In the 1800's most cities had a reservoir filled with water from nearby wells, which supplied the city with water. Hollow pine logs carried the water to each house—but the flow of water through these pipes was so small that fire engines had to be hooked up directly to the reservoirs or rivers. It was not until the 1870's that this problem was solved.

In 1874 a high-pressure water system was introduced to several cities in New York State. The cities built a pumping station near the source of their water supply. The pumping station forced water at high pressure into city pipes. Firefighters could now hook up hoses directly to hydrants in the city.

Modern Equipment

The complete modernization of firefighting equipment took place very quickly, from horse-drawn steam engines in the 1860's to gas motor engines in the 1920's. The use of new materials and chemicals and the building of skyscrapers have brought about changes in the way fires ignite, burn, travel, and have to be fought.

Today the fire department is one of the most important organizations in any community. Every department has at least two basic units—engine companies and ladder companies. Engine companies operate trucks and pumpers, which carry the pumps and hoses to put out the fire. Ladder companies use trucks with ladders on elevating platforms to rescue people who are trapped. Each works together as a team.

All firefighters wear special clothing, including a helmet to protect their heads from water, heat, and falling objects. They also wear waterproof and flame-retardant rubberized coats, pants, and boots, and special masks to protect them from harmful gases found in smoke.

Today there is a large variety of firefighting equipment. Some fire engines are actually boats that help put out blazes on ships and waterfront buildings. Fires can also be fought by air. Chemicals can be dropped from airplanes, and water can be scooped from a water source in large buckets and dropped on the fire. Even computers are now used in firefighting—they can transmit diagrams of floor plans and other useful information to the firemen. But the basic principles behind firefighting have not changed: Get to the fire quickly and try to keep it from spreading.

5

Forest Fires

The first area to be named a national reserve was Yellowstone National Park, in 1872. Then in 1891, after many devastating forest fires had destroyed hundreds of square miles of timberland, the U.S. Congress passed more laws meant to protect the nation's forests. All national parks were to be guarded by a Department of Forestry. This group would organize fire watches and teach fire prevention to tourists.

When President Theodore Roosevelt took office in 1901, he added over one quarter of the nation's remaining forests to the national park program. Lookout towers were built on the highest grounds, and foresters set up 24-hour watches—they believed that all fires had to be stopped, and the best way to do this was to act fast. Firefighters went into action at the slightest trace of smoke.

Smoke Jumpers

In the early 1920's, some daredevil airplane pilots suggested that planes could be used to fight forest fires. But almost everyone laughed at the idea of flying over a fire and actually parachuting into it—the idea just seemed too dangerous and impractical.

By 1939, however, airplanes had become safer, and a few test jumps were made by firefighters. They proved that given proper training and equipment, firemen *could* jump into a fire. This started the U.S. Smoke Jumper Program. On July 12, 1940, the first two smoke jumpers parachuted into the Nez Perce National Forest to put out a small forest fire.

In 1940 there were only twelve smoke jumpers. Today there are enough of them to populate smoke-jumping bases in Alaska, Washington, Idaho, Montana, Oregon, and California. For many, smoke-jumping is just a summer job, since that is when the risk of forest fires is highest. Smoke jumpers wear special jumpsuits with steel cages over their faces for protection, and they carry special safety lines to get down from any trees they may land in.

Aircraft of many types are used to fight forest fires, ranging from observation planes to helicopters to special-purpose aircraft. Helicopters can lay hose from the air faster than it can be dragged by men on the ground, and they can also be used to lift water-filled buckets from nearby lakes or streams. This can either be dumped on the fire or used to soak vegetation in the fire's path.

Supplies can also be dropped from airplanes to firefighters. Special honeycomb paper is first packed tightly into the bottom of tool cartons to absorb the shock of landing. (Honeycomb shock absorbers can also be used for dropping weapons, chainsaws, and even military vehicles.)

Over the years of fighting fires, scientists began to learn more about the forest. They realized that fire was not its enemy—instead, they began to consider fire as necessary to the forest's health as sunshine and rain.

Fires, it appeared, actually help the forest to develop—without them, the forest strangles and dies from lack of nutrients in the soil. Fire is nature's way of cleaning the forest floor of fallen trees, dead pine needles, and natural litter. When this dead plant life is burned, minerals are left in the ashes. Rain washes these minerals deep into the soil where the tree roots absorb them and grow.

Some seeds need high temperatures in order to sprout. Inside the cones of these trees are the seeds needed for new sprouts, but a *resin*, or sticky substance, keeps them sealed inside. Only under circumstances of extreme heat, such as a fire, will the resin melt and the seeds fall onto the ground.

Animals also thrive in burned-over areas. Some hawks are attracted to smoke: It tells them that their food—weasels and other small rodents—is on the run. Deer, elk, and bison find fire regrowth especially delicious and full of minerals and nutrients. Animals who eat this vegetation become stronger and healthier. Also wood smoke kills forest fungus and rids the forest of insects.

Scientists have found scars on trees proving that periodic fires were part of the normal cycle of the forest dating back to at least the 1600's. However, these scars stopped appearing around 1900, just about the same time the U.S. Forestry Department began fighting all forest fires.

So in 1972 park officials decided to allow fire to play its natural role in the health of the forest. This meant that firefighters would not fight natural fires —they would be allowed to go out themselves. Firemen would battle only blazes started by humans and those that endangered people or buildings.

However, once a forest fire starts, it can take on a life of its own. An uncontrolled fire can bring about so much destruction—such as burned roots—that regrowth may be very slow. A fire can turn a forest into a wasteland for a generation or longer. Sometimes the nutrients left on the forest floor escape into the atmosphere instead of returning to the soil. Escaping from a fire's path can make smaller wildlife easy prey for larger animals. So sometimes forest fires must be fought.

Even then, a forest fire can turn into a disaster. The Yellowstone fire of 1988 was one of those.

Black Saturday in Yellowstone

The summer of 1988 was an unusually hot one in much of the United States. In June, lightning started over 48 fires in Yellowstone and the surrounding forests. Many of these were allowed to burn, and some of them did die out quickly by themselves. However, by July things began to look bad. There had been little rainfall, so the park was very dry. And winds were making the remaining fires grow dangerously fast.

By July 21 almost 17,000 acres had burned, and park officials decided to fight all the fires in the park. The next day one started in Idaho's Targhee National Forest—only 200 yards away from Yellowstone—because a careless woodcutter had left behind a burning cigarette. This fire quickly spread to Yellowstone.

By August the fires were still going strong and spreading daily. The flames roared up the trunks of lodgepole pine trees, splitting them in half. When these burning trees exploded, bits of flaming needles and branches, called *firebrands,* flew through the air and ignited new blazes as far as half a mile in front of the fire.

The fire was advancing as much as 5 to 10 miles a day. Winds blew at gale forces, and flames 200 feet tall leaped across the forest. As news of the fires grew, people started to wonder why they couldn't be put out. Over 9,000 firefighters were called to help, including soldiers from the U.S. Army and Merchant Marines. Helicopters and airplanes dropped millions of gallons of water and chemicals on the fires. The firemen worked day and night clearing underbrush and trees away so there would be nothing left to burn. They sprayed fire retardant foam and wet down buildings.

But the flames just wouldn't give up. On August 20, later called Black Sunday, 80-mile-per-hour, hurricane-force gusts of wind whipped up every fire that was burning. On that day alone, the blaze destroyed over 160,000 acres—more land than had been destroyed by fire at one time in the last 116 years.

By September the blaze had reached the geyser area of northwest Wyoming, Old Faithful Village. It threatened to destroy the small village where a historic inn built in 1903 was located. Tourists were quickly evacuated, and firefighters turned on sprinkler systems and drenched rooftops with retardant foam. At 3:30 p.m. Old Faithful erupted, just as the fire reached the end of the woods. Embers the size of golf balls flew through the air, igniting cabins. For more than an hour the fire burned around the village, and then leaped to the other side. When the smoke cleared, over 20 buildings, mainly cabins, were destroyed. But most of the village, including the inn, survived.

The fire, called the Hellroaring Fire by some, lasted for three more days—but on September 11 it started to snow. Slowly the falling snow and rains began to put out the fires—after almost two months! Altogether the fires burned nearly a million acres of the 2.2 million-acre park. But in the spring of 1989 the forest began to grow. Roots of bushes had not been destroyed by the fire. Lodgepole pinecones had burst open in the heat and the seeds survived in the soil. Pine sprouts appeared out of the ashes.

Grasses, aspens, berry bushes, and wildflowers all began to grow in rich, burned soil.

Out of the ruins of the charred old forest a healthy new forest is sprouting. The landscape may be different, but the forest is flourishing. The beauty of Yellowstone National Park remains.

6

Fire Disasters in the Air

The *Hindenburg* Horror

In 1937 the *Hindenburg* made its maiden voyage from Frankfurt, Germany, to the United States. It was a rigid cigar-shaped airship known as a *zeppelin* or a *dirigible*. Since 1936 dirigibles had crossed the Atlantic safely over ten times. No one had any reason to fear airships—they were an exciting new type of transportation.

The *Hindenburg* was 803 feet long and traveled at a speed of 84 miles per hour. Able to fly in any weather, it could remain in the air for an 8,000-mile journey. What made the *Hindenburg* stay afloat were sixteen bags filled with a very explosive gas called hydrogen. Because of this danger, every precaution was taken to ensure the safety of the passengers and crew. Smoking was not allowed on board. Crew members who had to go near the hydrogen-filled bags wore padded shoes so that they wouldn't create static electricity. Even the walkways were padded.

The *Hindenburg* was the luxury airship of its day.

Americans, Germans, and other passengers paid $400 each to ride on it—a fortune in 1937. The airship had 25 staterooms, dining rooms, a cocktail lounge with a piano, and room for 100 passengers. At certain altitudes, people could even open the windows for a breath of fresh air.

On May 3, 97 passengers and 61 crew members boarded the *Hindenburg* in Frankfurt. Carefree, they danced and dined for three fun-filled days. On the evening of May 6, spectators and the ground crew waited at the U.S. Naval Air Station in Lakehurst, New Jersey, for the airship to land. The landing had been delayed for almost 13 hours because of thunderstorms in the area.

When the captain got the go-ahead to land it was after 7:00. At 7:25 p.m. the ship descended to 200 feet from the ground and dropped its mooring lines. Without warning there was a sudden flash of light, as bright as the sun at noon, and the airship burst into flames. The back of the *Hindenburg* tilted, sending the nose up into the air.

Passengers who were watching from windows continued to wave to crowds below, unaware of the danger. When they finally realized what was happening, they began to jump out in a panic—some slid down the mooring ropes. Miraculously, passengers in the front of the airship were able to escape by jumping, though many were injured. Within minutes all that was left of the *Hindenburg* was a skeleton frame. Twenty-two crewmen, thirteen passengers, and one ground man died. The remains of the airship were sent back to Germany, where they were eventually melted down to be used as frames for German planes during World War II.

The cause of the disaster will probably never be known. Some say that a spark of lightning may have ignited the hydrogen. Others say the *Hindenburg* was sabotaged—that a bomb planted by the German Nazi government caused the explosion. Whatever the cause, zeppelins have never again been flown.

The *Challenger* Explosion

On the morning of January 28, 1986, a crowd assembled at Cape Canaveral air force base in Florida to watch the lift-off of the *Challenger* space shuttle. The *Challenger*'s mission was unique—it was the first time a civilian would join the astronauts being launched into space. A third-grade teacher from New Hampshire, 37-year-old Christa McAuliffe, was on the shuttle. She planned to beam back science lessons from space to children all over the country.

The weather that morning was unusually cold. The *Challenger* had already been delayed on four previous occasions, and everyone was now anxious to see it actually take off. Television cameras were broadcasting the lift-off live. All over the United States, children watched excitedly from their classrooms.

That morning patches of ice and icicles covered

parts of the shuttle, but most of them were soon cleared away by a special ice team. Still, some officials warned that there was no way to predict where flying ice would land when the shuttle was launched —they were afraid the ice could cause damage to the *Challenger*. For more than three hours the situation was checked and rechecked. Finally the crew was given the word to prepare for lift-off.

At 11:38 a.m. everyone in the grandstands screamed "Go!" as the rocket was launched into the air. Just 73 seconds later, when the shuttle was 10 miles high and 8 miles downrange from the launchpad, traveling at 1,977 miles per hour, it exploded.

Mission Control went silent. Then a single announcement was made that a "major malfunction" had occurred. Those who watched it on television and in person remember seeing a tiny orange flame flicker, and then a gigantic explosion as the *Challenger* broke up in pieces and fell back to Earth.

After the explosion the nation mourned the seven crew members. The students at Christa McAuliffe's school in New Hampshire had watched the takeoff on TV. They had been wearing party hats and shaking noisemakers. Christa's parents had been watching from the launch site, as were her husband, Steven, and her children, 9-year-old Scott and 6-year-old Caroline. The whole country was shocked and saddened by the tragedy they saw.

The investigation of the *Challenger* disaster revealed that the seals of the rocket boosters were to blame—the *O-rings* of the seals had been affected by the cold overnight temperatures. When the craft took off, its booster tanks held 500,000 gallons of highly explosive liquid hydrogen and oxygen. A small spark ignited these tanks, which were no longer sealed because of these faulty O-rings. NASA and the manufacturer had known about the problem of the O-rings before takeoff, but they didn't think it was serious.

The *Hindenburg* and *Challenger* have gone down in history. Both were examples of the most advanced and amazing modern know-how of their day. But both were destroyed by the power of fire.

7

Fire as a Weapon

As soon as man was able to make fire, he used it as a weapon. The first fire weapon was the flaming arrow shot at the enemy's houses and crops. The Romans created a weapon called the *springald*. It released hundreds of fire darts that set enemy towns ablaze. The main purpose of both of these weapons was to cause panic and confusion so it would be easier to attack the enemy.

The Bombing of Europe

One of the first fire weapons of the twentieth century was the flamethrower, which was used first in World War I. The flamethrower sent out a spray or stream of a special gasoline mixture. A pilot light at the end of the nozzle set the liquid on fire. The gasoline was carried in a canister on a soldier's back.

During World War II, the death of hundreds of thousands of people and the destruction of millions of dollars of property were caused by a new weapon of war—firebombs, or *incendiaries*. When a firebomb is dropped from an aircraft, it does not destroy buildings with a big bang. Instead, it explodes in such a way that large burning fragments scatter over a wide area. Just one bomb can set a whole block of buildings on fire.

The firebomb was first used by the German air force in World War II in air attacks over Poland and later over England. The Germans were sent out to drop bombs over Polish and English cities to cause uncontrollable fires.

Enormous numbers of their aircraft dropped thousands of firebombs night after night on English cities. On December 29, 1940, German firebombing started 1,500 fires in London alone. Yet the people of London did not give up—they put out the fires day after day and somehow survived.

The Allies then used these same bombs on the Germans. The most severe attacks were made on the cities of Dresden and Cologne. When the bombing was over, in 1945, Dresden was completely devastated. In Cologne an estimated 70,000 people were killed in one night. Eventually the bridges and over 80 percent of the buildings were destroyed. The original layout of the city's streets was buried under the rubble of so many collapsed buildings that it was lost.

The destruction from the firebombs was so severe because of the firestorms they created. A *firestorm* is the result of several fires breaking out at once in the same area, where there is no wind to draw them in any one direction. The flames then draw up together, as in a furnace. This draws the air around the fires to the center at a speed of over 100 miles per hour.

The heat in a firestorm is so intense that nothing can survive. Underground shelters become useless. Even the oxygen inside these shelters is eaten up by the fire, leaving a *vacuum,* a place with no air to breathe. The people inside suffocate. No fire department in the world has yet found a way to stop a firestorm.

The city of Warsaw, Poland, experienced a firestorm. The fire was so intense that it sucked in vast amounts of air from every direction. Soon hurricane-force winds blew along the streets. Near the fire, the winds were so strong that people were blown over and sucked into the fire.

The Kuwait Oil Fires

Forty-six years after the firebombs of World War II, fire was used as a very different kind of weapon.

On August 1, 1990, Iraq invaded the oil-rich country of Kuwait and started the Persian Gulf War. The United States and its allies began bombing Iraq on January 16, 1991. In February, U.S. and allied troops entered Kuwait to free the country from Iraqi rule. As the Iraqis retreated in defeat from the U.S.-led forces, they blew up many of Kuwait's oil wells.

When the wells exploded, the *caps,* or tops, of the wells were blown off, and the oil pouring out of them caught fire. Those who saw the oil fires described them as a raging inferno.

It took 10,000 workers from 34 countries 125,000 tons of heavy equipment to put out the fires and to put the caps back on the wells. The firefighters were organized into well-capping teams of eight or nine men. The teams included a supervisor, a heavy-equipment specialist, a paramedic, four explosion specialists, and one or two other workers to monitor poisonous gases. They worked 12-hour days, 28 days in a row, and then went home for a 4-week rest. Their employers charged the Kuwaiti government $500,000 a month for each team, adding up to a total of about $2 billion.

The firefighters had to work close to the wells. Some wells had 250-foot-high geysers of flame roaring above them, and the temperatures often reached 650 degrees.

Several methods were used to put out the oil fires. Some crews fought them mainly with the help of *potassium bicarbonate,* a dry chemical compound that resembles baking soda—it works by robbing the fire of oxygen. Crews in Kuwait used trucks similar to those used by our local fire departments to pump the chemical on the blazing oil at a rate of 200 pounds per second.

Another method was to dig near the oil wells, creating reservoirs that were able to hold up to a million gallons of water from the Persian Gulf. Then the team hit the fire with four streams of water at once. By doing this, they were able to put out a fire in half an hour.

When water failed, the firefighting team resorted to dynamite. The team supervisor packed 200 pounds of dynamite into a 55-gallon barrel; then the barrel was wrapped in insulating material and soaked with water. Last they attached a 75-foot boom to a bulldozer and dangled the barrel from the end of the boom. When the barrel was above the gap between the wellhead and the bottom of the flame, it was ignited—the explosion sucked out all the oxygen and put out the fire.

The work was very dangerous. Workers wore goggles to protect their eyes, but the constant spray of water usually made the goggles impossible to see through. However, workers who refused to wear them took the chance of temporary blindness if the oil got into their eyes. Two other constant concerns for the firefighters were getting clean and keeping cool—they had to take frequent baths in man-made pools filled with sea water.

On November 8, 1991, much earlier than anyone had expected, the fires were all out—it had taken only 8 months! Seven men were dead, and seven were injured. The complete effect of the fires on the environment is still unknown. Air was polluted, water was contaminated, and wildlife died. Most of the oil burned, but some spread across the desert. Part of this evaporated in the fire and heat, and part formed a tarry asphalt.

Today many of the wells have been put back to work and are producing oil for sale around the world.

8

Fire Prevention

America may very well have some of the fastest fire departments in the world, and some of the best equipment—but we also have the poorest record in establishing fire prevention programs. More Americans die in fires each year than do people in any other country—and the majority of the people who die are children.

Home Fire-Prevention Equipment

Many fires would never have developed if they had been detected in time. Therefore, every home should have smoke detectors. Ideally one should be placed on every level of a house—the first and second floors, the attic, and the basement—and in every separate sleeping area. Ask your parents to check the batteries in the smoke detectors frequently.

When fires are small, they can be easily handled with a small home fire extinguisher. There are a variety of extinguishers, the newest of which is a push-button unit that fits into a handy wall bracket that can be hung near the stove, fireplace, or furnace. When you press the button, it shoots out a 25-foot stream of liquid that can extinguish all types of fires, including gasoline, oil, and grease fires.

A recently invented safety device that may soon be available for use in homes as well as in public buildings is the Baker Life Chute, designed by Ralph Baker. A nylon mesh contraption that looks something like a giant stocking, it can be attached to windows in buildings up to 20 floors high and used as an escape tunnel when there is a fire. A person simply climbs through a window or from the rooftop and slides feet first through the chute, all the way to the ground. The flexible curve of the chute acts like a brake and slows down the person's speed.

Expert Advice

The U.S. Fire Administration says that each American is likely to be involved in three fires during his or her lifetime. Knowing what to do, and remaining calm, can save your life. Here is some advice given by the experts.

1. Leave immediately. Do not try to fight a fire, not even a small one, without the help of an adult. But do ask your parents to keep a box or two of baking soda on hand for small grease fires.
2. Never open a door if it feels hot. Try another escape route or wait for help.

3. Crawl on the floor when you go through smoky areas. The air closer to the floor is cooler and easier to breathe—hot air rises toward the ceiling.

4. Do not run if your clothes catch fire. Roll on the floor to smother the flames. Fire experts call this "Stop, Drop, and Roll."

5. Do not return to the burning building—even if you've forgotten something. If a person or animal has been left behind, tell a firefighter about it.

If you want more information, call your local fire department. Learn their telephone number and write it down near your phone. If you see someone playing with fire, tell an adult. If you are in a fire, stay cool and follow a prearranged drill. You and your family should start practicing such a drill now —*before* a fire starts. By practicing fire prevention, you may save your own life, or someone else's.

Other titles in the Explorer Books series